THE HOW AND WHY WONDER® BOOK OF
SNAKES

WRITTEN BY GEORG ZAPPLER
DIRECTOR, STATEN ISLAND ZOO
ILLUSTRATED BY DOUGAL MacDOUGAL

⊠ ALLAN PUBLISHERS, INC.
Exclusive Distributors

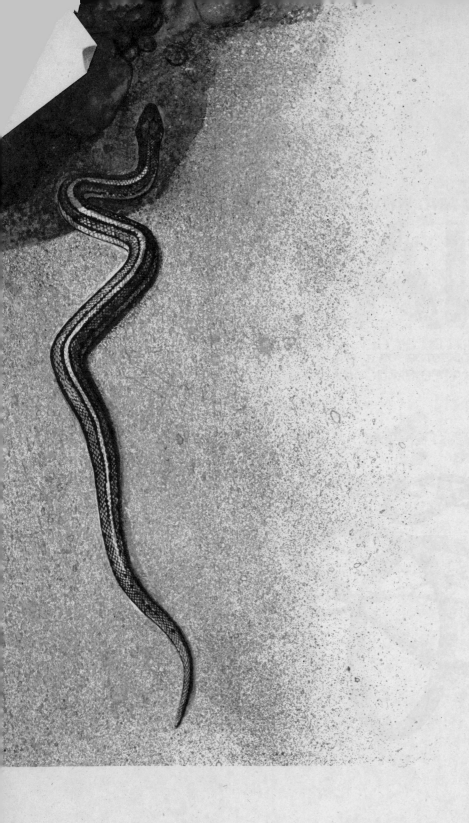

1981 Printing

Cover Copyright © 1981 GROSSET & DUNLAP, INC.
Text Copyright © 1975 by Grosset & Dunlap, Inc.
Illustrations Copyright © 1969 by the Hamlyn Publishing Group Ltd.
Illustrations originally published in the Grosset All-Color Guide Series.
All rights reserved.
Published simultaneously in Canada.   Printed in the United States of America.
Published by GROSSET & DUNLAP, Inc.
Exclusively distributed by Allan Publishers, Inc.
How and Why Wonder® Books is a trademark of GROSSET & DUNLAP, INC.
ISBN: 0-8241-5073-2

Contents

A cylindrical skink (top) and a slowworm (below), two of a number of lizards that have evolved as snakelike in appearance.

Eastern Collared Lizard

The belly scales of the lizard (left) show no change in structure. The pattern continues along the body without a break. A single row of scales on the bottom surface of snakes is specially adapted to their movements.

Snakes and Their Relatives

The world we live in contains a vast

What is a reptile? array of animals: large ones, small ones, fat ones, and slim ones — animals that fly and animals that swim. Every portion of the earth has its own animal inhabitants. Some animals have spinal columns to give strength and flexibility to the body; they are called "vertebrates." Fish, amphibians, reptiles, birds, and mammals are all vertebrates, and so one could say that snakes are related to trout, frogs, canaries and dogs. But they bear a closer resemblance to turtles, crocodiles and lizards because they all have a common ancestry. Thus, they are quite similar in many of their bodily structures. Scientists have put them into a group or class called "reptiles," separate from all other classes. Reptiles have scales, breathe air, lay shelled eggs, and depend upon outside sources for their body heat. Some of these characteristics are shared with one or another of the vertebrate classes, but reptiles are the only ones in which all four occur.

Many sorts of reptiles exist. Over 6,000 species are scattered throughout the world. 3,000 of them are snakes. Most live in warm places, but there are some reptiles living in the colder parts as well. Reptiles are frequently thought of as dangerous, but actually only a few species of snakes and lizards are poisonous. Most reptiles are harmless and, indeed, are extremely beneficial to man because they feed on rodents and insect pests. Many are beautiful and all are interesting to observe.

The First Snakes

When did the first snakes appear? Snakes have been on earth for about 125 million years. This seems to be a very long time, but actually they are a young group, the most recently evolved of all reptiles. Reptile history goes back 260 million years. And what a glorious history it has been! Huge dinosaurs, strange flying reptiles, and wild-looking sea serpents once dominated the world. In this exotic "Age of Reptiles" the snake had no part. Only after the dinosaurs became extinct did the snake make its appearance. When small mammals became widespread, preying snakes evolved from lizard ancestors.

How did the first snakes evolve? There is some disagreement among scientists as to just how lizards gave rise to snakes. One theory is that some ancient lizards took to a burrowing existence. In deep, underground tunnels, legs were of little use, and so they were forfeited in exchange for a long, muscular body, capable of sinuous movement. Other underground adaptations took place. The size and shape of the eye and the lack of an external ear are of definite advantage. To a burrowing animal, eyes without movable eyelides are beneficial, and external ear openings with eardrums serve no function. Millions of years later, when some snakes returned to surface life, they appeared with their limbless burrowing adaptations completed. The first ground-living snakes were large, constrictor types. It was only much later that the smaller kinds that are common today evolved. Poisonous snakes were the last to evolve.

It is interesting that the snake's evolution took place at a time when other reptiles had retired in favor of the mammals. That they have succeeded throughout the difficult "Age of Mammals" is due to their extraordinary adaptations and their way of life. They are secretive animals, hiding in foliage and rocks, burrowing underground or retreating into water. This has saved them from large fierce mammal predators which would have undoubtedly caused their extinction otherwise.

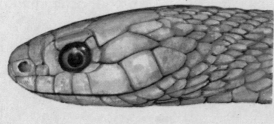

There is no eyelid on the head of the snake (top), but the lizard (below) has one, as well as an external ear.

The Snake's Body

Snakes and lizards are usually classified together in a single order called the squamata. If one thinks of a typical lizard and a typical snake, this seems odd. But there are lizards without legs. There are even lizards without eardrums. Some burrowing lizards have the sort of eye shield usually associated with snakes. (This device, useful for keeping dirt out of the eyes, is a transparent, round spectacle derived from body scales.) Although most snakes have a single row of scales on the belly, some have several rows, as do all lizards. However, comparing all features, such as eyes, ears and belly, on any given pair of snake and lizard, you are unlikely to find more than one confusing characteristic, and proper identification can be made.

How do snakes differ from lizards?

All vertebrates have internal organs quite similar to those of other vertebrates. Snakes, however, because of their long, narrow bodies, have evolved an unusual arrangement of organs. Instead of coiled intestines, for instance, snakes have a straight canal that passes from the mouth to the vent with but a single loop in the small intestine. The stomach is merely an enlarged portion of the gut. Organs that come in pairs, such as lungs and kidneys, are arranged one on either side in other vertebrates. Snakes, however, do not have room for this sort

How are the snake's organs arranged?

of symmetry. Thus, the kidneys are found one behind the other, right one first. Most snakes have only one lung, the right one. Those with two have the left one poorly developed. The lung usually extends more than half the length of the body. In the reproductive organs, the one on the right is usually larger than the left one. The liver is very long with a small left lobe. The gall bladder of a snake does not appear in the customary vertebrate position, next to the liver, but is squeezed in below it. The bladder is nonexistent.

Just as the snake's internal organs are uniquely arranged, its skeleton is also highly adapted. The skull is greatly modified for feeding (see page 13). With no legs, there need be no modifications of the vertebrae for their attachment. Each vertebra looks very much like the next one, except for the first one or two behind the skull. Most remarkable is the number of vertebrae in the backbone — the total ranges from 180 to 400, depending on species.

What does a snake's skeleton look like?

The snake appears to be almost all tail with a head at one end. However, only that part of the spinal column behind the vent or "cloaca" can be rightfully called a tail. This part is relatively short. Most snakes have a double row of scales beneath the tail, which is the clue to its location.

Where does the tail begin?

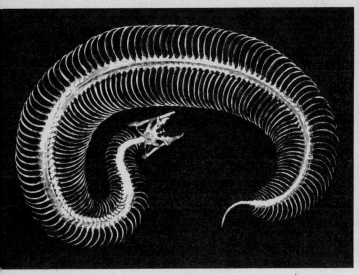

Snake skeleton

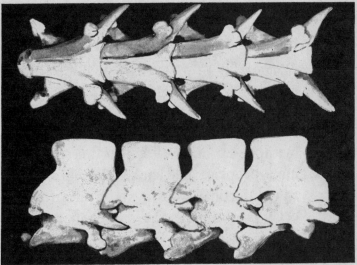

Snake vertebrae viewed from the bottom (top illustration) and the side (lower illustration).

Snakes, of course, have a special problem in movement, different from animals with legs. To achieve real efficiency in wriggling through life, tremendous flexibility is necessary. The large number of vertebrae is of great importance. It makes the spinal column strong with less possibility of damage to the spinal chord. Each vertebra interlocks with the next in a ball-and-socket manner. Various projections and prongs stretch from vertebra to vertebra. Thus, each vertebra articulates with the next at five points, making strong joints capable of withstanding great stress. Each joint bends only a few degrees in a vertical direction, but the combination of many such joints gives the snake its flexibility.

How does a snake move?

Complicated muscles range down either side of the backbone. These are shortened on one side of the body with contractions beginning at the head and moving backward along the entire length of the snake. Then a wave of contraction is sent down the other side of the body. Not all muscles on either side are contracted at the same time. This throws the body into horizontal waves, called undulations, the muscles pulling first to one side, then to the other.

If a snake should be placed on a piece of smooth glass, all these undulations would get it nowhere. A rough texture to push against is necessary to locomotion. Small irregularities on the surface of the ground help the snake to move. As the undulations move down the snake, the outer and rear parts of each body loop come into contact with these bumps. This resistance is enough to stop the backward movement of the loop. As the snake is exerting muscular effort, part of the body is propelled forward. Thus, while each loop remains stationary in relation to the ground, the tail moves steadily along the track left by the head.

Long thin snakes move more efficiently because they have more body loops, which means more points pushing against the ground.

Most snakes move in a side-to-side undulating way, but some use another method. A kind of concertina movement propels some snakes through burrows. Vertical loops at the front of the body press against the wall of the track and grip tight as the rear is drawn forward. Then the rear end is looped vertically and pressed against the walls as the front straightens and moves forward.

Some desert snakes have a special form of locomotion known as sidewinding. Loose sand makes it impossible for the snake to get a proper grip with customary undulations, so sidewinders push downward rather than horizontally. A loop of the front end of the snake is thrown forward, while the neck is placed on the ground. The rest of the body twists, rises above the ground, and lands in front of the head and neck. The fore part touches the ground first, followed shortly thereafter by middle and tail. Long before the tail touches the ground, the head and neck have been thrown forward and sideways once again. In this manner, only two short lengths of the snake's body touch the ground at any time. This gives an appearance of sideways-spiraling and leaves a series of tracks shaped like a capital J. The crook marks the position of the neck, and the stem is made by the body coming forward. The cross at the top is the tail's mark as it pushes clear of the ground.

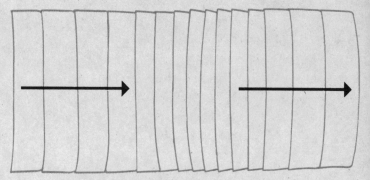

Heavy snakes moving forward use their belly scales as indicated by this illustration.

Snakes with thick bodies frequently use another method of travel. Here the body is kept in a straight line. A belly scale is pulled forward with muscles attached to the ribs. Another muscle pulls the scale backward. The hind edge then catches the ground and propels the snake forward. One after another, the belly scales are moved and the snake slowly creeps forward.

Most snakes are able to use all these methods of progression as the need arises. Even water snakes can sidewind on sand, if necessary.

Snakes can, in addition, swim, climb, and "fly." Swimming is a natural offshoot of crawling, since the same undulating movements are used. Using a modified concertina action, a snake can work its way up a tree. Those that climb particularly well have special belly scales to assist them. Some snakes that live in trees are able to leap from tree to tree. They hold their bodies parallel to the ground so that resistance to the air breaks the speed of the fall. The body is flattened or even concave along the belly. In such a leap, the snake actually seems to be flying.

Ordinarily, a snake travels very slowly. Only in a great emergency is

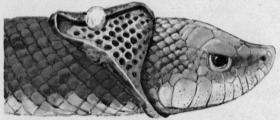

Before shedding its skin, a snake has a milky appearance. Fluid covers the eye (top illustration). Eventually, the skin begins to split at the edge of the lips and the snake begins to wriggle out of it (bottom illustration).

The snake wriggles out of its old skin, which turns inside-out (left). The skin usually comes off in one piece (right).

speed employed, and then for just a short distance.

A very special sort of skin is necessary to a snake. It must be **What is snake skin?** smooth enough to avoid resistance to forward movement and rough enough to grip and push against obstacles. It must be flexible but tough. Thus, the snake evolved a skin of overlapping scales with the free edges pointing toward the rear. Scales are tough enough not to wear out and smooth enough to offer no resistance to moving forward. They are not wet or slimy.

Snake scales are formed of folded skin. Thinner pleats of folded skin are found between the scales. On the belly the folds are simple, but on the back they are more complicated. This arrangement of scales and folds permits flexibility of the snake's body-covering and allows for utmost distension.

The outer covering of a snake's skin gets replaced at intervals. When this happens, the snake appears cloudy or milky, due to a thin layer of fluid separating the old skin from the new one forming beneath. When the new covering is completely formed, the old one is shed. Beginning at the corner of the lips, the snake works the old skin off in one piece, turning it inside out in the process. The shed skin is a perfect cast of the snake it used to fit.

Snakes look most beautiful immediately after shedding. The new skin shows its colors most brilliantly and the patterns shimmer forth in all their complexity.

Snake Senses

How do snakes see?

Snakes have all the senses people have and a few others besides. There are differences in the structure of the sense organs and their functions. Snake eyes are different from any other animal's. They have spectacles instead of eyelids. Snakes do not change focus, as others do, by using muscles to alter the shape of the lens. They have round lenses which do not easily alter in shape, so they move the lens forward to change the focus. The lens is yellow and works as a color filter. Unlike their cousins, the lizards, snakes have double cones in their retinas, as well as rods, allowing sharpness of color vision.

Snakes are shortsighted. When a sharp image is desired by most animals, a portion of the retina, called the fovea, is employed. Here many cones are packed together. But most snakes lack the fovea and so go through life with dull vision, never really seeing small details. As the eyes are at the sides of the head, it is difficult for the average snake to judge distance. Snakes, however, have exceptional use of the sort of vision we have only at the sides of our eyes, resulting in a keen perception of any sort of movement. Few snakes are able to locate or recognize prey that is motionless, but any movement will attract their attention.

A few tree snakes have an area of the retina similar to the fovea of other animals. These snakes can sight down grooves in the snout for forward vision.

They have long, horizontal pupils, shaped like keyholes above their long, pointed snouts. The pupil is extended more toward the front margin of the eye, giving such snakes binocular vision.

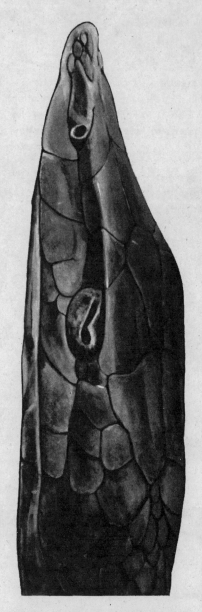

The tree snake is one of the few snakes able to see things sharply.

10

Snakes have no eardrum or middle ear.

What is the ear like? As you might suspect, this absence has a notable effect on the sense of hearing. They do have a functioning inner ear that connects with a bone at the rear end of the snake's jaw. It allows the snake to pick up vibrations from the ground and thus to "hear" movements of other animals and even inanimate objects disturbed by wind or water. The snake's ears are sensitive to nearby sounds against the ground, but almost useless in picking up warnings transmitted through the air. On rare occasions, when the volume of sound is enough to set the ground vibrating or when the frequency is low, snakes can pick up distant, airborne sounds.

The snake's inner ear, like that of a human, helps in maintaining balance. This ability is particularly evident in snakes, as can be noted from watching a snake moving freely along slender tree branches or resting on a wire fence.

Sight and hearing may be of small use

How do snakes smell and taste? to a snake as distance-senses, but smell makes up for the lack, because snakes, in addition to big, well-equipped nostrils supplied with all the normal sensory equipment, have an additional smelling organ. Within the mouth is an area known as Jacobson's organ — a pair of cavities lined with a membrane similar to that found in the smelling portion of the nose. Jacobson's organ works cooperatively with the tongue, which is long and forked. Some people mistakenly believe that the flickering tongue of a snake is a stinging mechanism, but the tongue is harmless to us and very useful to the snake as a special smelling organ. As the tongue flicks out of the mouth, it picks up tiny, invisible particles from the air or ground. These are carried by the tongue to Jacobson's organ, where they are analyzed. The information thus gained allows the snake to trail its prey, find a mate, and check on objects in the immediate surroundings. That is why the tongue is so constantly in motion when a snake is exploring. This modification, however, deprived the snake somewhat in the area of taste. There are few taste buds in the forked tongue.

Snakes, like us, have small sensory endings all over the skin.

How does the sense of touch work? In spite of the scales, the entire surface of a snake is sensitive to touch. There are other touch receivers, as well, in many snakes. Small circular areas, barely visible to the naked eye, are found near the tips of the scales on the back and flanks. These are richly provided with nerve endings that are employed in the important business of receiving and transmitting information from touch. They may also be heat receptors to detect variations in temperature, an important factor for "cold-blooded" snakes. All the pit vipers, including rattlesnakes, have special heat-receptor organs located in pits next to their nostrils that enable them to locate warm-blooded prey in the dark. Many boas and pythons have smaller pits that line their lips.

Cold-Bloodedness

Snakes are said to be "cold-blooded," which does not mean they are cold, but that they cannot control their own temperature and keep it at a constant level, as do birds and mammals. The surroundings of a snake determine its temperature — if the day and the place are warm, the snake will be warm. In a cold place its temperature is low.

What does "cold-blooded" mean?

Animals' bodies function well only when they are warm. Since the snake is dependent upon its environment for heat, it is more likely to choose locations where heat is constant. More species of snakes can be found in the tropics than anywhere else in the world. A few do live in cool, temperate areas, but none exist in the polar regions.

Why do most snakes live in warm regions?

Although snakes cannot generate much heat within their body tissues, they can move from place to place to provide warmth. In the cooler parts of their range, snakes can be found frequently basking in the sun. Basking, combined with exercise, may give a snake a temperature slightly higher than its surroundings. If a snake becomes too warm, it will move into the shade. A snake will die if it becomes too hot or too cool, but it can survive by moving to the right places.

Do snakes have any means of controlling their temperature?

Dark colors absorb heat faster than light ones — and so, generally, snakes from cold climates have darker hues.

Really big snakes are found only in the tropics, because their huge bodies would take so long to get warm in temperate areas that there would be no time left for such vital activities as hunting.

How does size and color influence temperature?

Those snakes that live in temperate regions cannot survive the cold of winter. Even if they didn't immediately freeze to death, their cold bodies would be so slowed down that any predator could make short work of them. To avoid this, snakes retreat below the ground or into a hole within a hollow tree, there to sleep away the winter, removed from frost. Sometimes many snakes will retreat to the same sleeping place, called a hibernaculum.

Why do snakes hibernate?

A hibernaculum — the retreat of many snakes in winter.

Snake Food

What do snakes eat?
All snakes are carnivorous. There are no vegetarian snakes and very few will touch carrion. Most snakes will eat only prey that has been seen to move. Each species has its own food preference. Some eat frogs, others lizards, quite a number prefer rodents, and there are those that eat only other snakes. Snakes that hunt by night patrol suitable places for finding prey. Most day-hunters lurk in hiding, lunging forward at the right moment. Some lure their prey with brightly colored tails, waved appealingly toward the victim.

How can a snake devour large prey?
A snake's long, slim body and head would seem to suggest very small prey, but a snake can consume animals that are proportionately very large because its skin is stretchy. It also has a remarkably hinged jaw that can be opened so wide that it can swallow a meal two or three times the diameter of its own head.

A snake's teeth are pointed and well designed for keeping a tight grip on prey during feeding. They are not used for chewing. The prey is worked through the jaws into the muscles of the throat. The time taken to swallow a large animal may be considerable — as much as an hour. During this time, with the snake's mouth and throat filled to capacity, special muscles carry the windpipe forward over the tongue so that it projects beyond the mouth. This allows

Frogs are a common prey of many snakes. Illustrated here is an Old World watersnake.

the snake to continue breathing during the long swallow.

Digestion begins in the mouth with the production of saliva. Even some harmless snakes have mildly poisonous venom that kills and begins digestion before the food is swallowed.

13

Baby Snakes

How do snakes court? When a female snake is ready to breed, a special scent is produced by her glands. With flickering tongue, the male picks up the scent trail and follows the female. Once together, a ritual courtship follows. In many cases, the male will rub his chin along the back and sides of the female, constantly flicking his tongue. Special touch receptors in the male's chin will establish whether the female is of the same species. If she is not, courtship is discontinued. Otherwise, the male will gradually work his way forward, nodding his head and rubbing his chin against her, until he reaches the nape of her neck. Then he throws a loop of the rear part of his body across her back and their tails intertwine. Most females remain passive during courtship, but in some species, both sexes engage in a nuptial dance. Frequently two male snakes will engage in a combat dance very similar to the nuptial dance. Intertwined, they sway and press against each other, rising higher and higher off the ground until one gives way and flees. No snake is ever seriously injured in these duels.

How do snakes mate? When the courting ritual has been completed, the female snake opens her cloaca. The male inserts his penis and sperm is transferred into her body. The penis of a snake is a double structure. Only one half, called a hemipene, is used at a time. Sometimes it is covered with spines that lock it into the female, so that even if she should

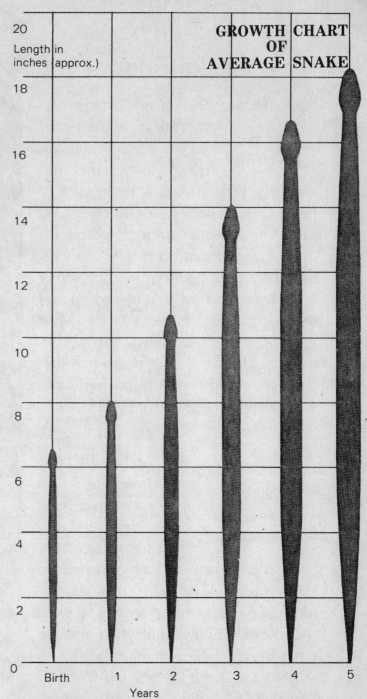

GROWTH CHART OF AVERAGE SNAKE

Length in inches (approx.)

Years — Birth, 1, 2, 3, 4, 5

begin to move away, mating is always completed.

Snake eggs have shells like thick parchment. This protects the young snake while allowing moisture and oxygen to enter. Inside the egg, yolk provides ample food for the developing young.

How are snake eggs constructed?

14

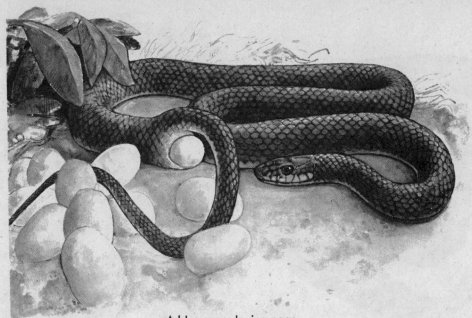

A blue racer laying eggs.

Most female snakes deposit their eggs in shallow holes.

Where are the eggs laid? These may be in the crevices of rocks or in the ground. Once laid, the eggs will be covered with a thin layer of soil which hides them from enemies and stabilizes the temperature. After careful selection of the nesting site and proper attention to temperature control, the mother usually moves away, allowing the environment to care for the developing young.

The incubation period varies considerably. It depends in

When do the eggs hatch? part on when the eggs were laid. Some snakes lay shortly after mating; others may wait for months. If the time within the mother's body is prolonged, the embryo is well on its way to full development, requiring a much shorter period in the egg in the outside world. Temperature also is a factor. The warmer the surroundings, the faster the embryo will develop.

When the baby snake is large enough to hatch, a small pointed tooth (called an egg-tooth) on the tip of its upper jaw comes into use. This cuts through the tough shell. Having served its purpose, the egg-tooth then drops off.

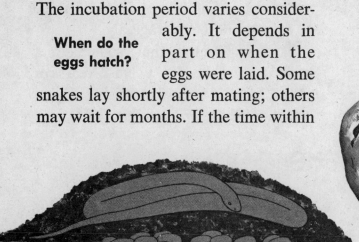

King cobras make a mound as a nest for their eggs.

Most snakes are oviparous (egg-laying). The baby snake actually cuts itself out of its shell by means of an "egg-tooth."

Python with eggs.

A few snakes give birth to living young.

Most species of snakes do lay eggs, but

Do all baby snakes come from eggs? some give birth to living young. Of these, only a very few have a placenta such as that of mammals, although simpler. The others just hold their eggs within them until the young are ready to hatch. The embryos within have been feeding from the yolk just as they would outside the mother's body. In those instances where a simple placenta does exist, food is transmitted from the mother's body.

Mostly, snakes that lay eggs have larger litters than those that bear live young. No female snakes are able to feed their young after birth and few demonstrate any sort of parental care. The babies are so well developed at birth that they are quite able to fend for themselves.

Young snakes grow rapidly. Rattle-

When do snakes become mature? snakes double their birth length during the first year; some pythons even triple it. A great deal depends upon the species, the climate, and the available food. In later years, snakes grow more slowly, but some growth occurs throughout life. Sexual maturity varies from one year to six years, depending on species, with three to four years the average age.

It is estimated that some larger snakes can live for twenty years or more. Smaller species probably do not live more than ten or fifteen years.

Enemies of Snakes

Most snakes' enemies are creatures that

Why do snakes have enemies? prey upon them as a source of food. Some, such as the mongoose, the meerkat, and the hedge-hog, can even devour poisonous snakes because they are partially immune to the venom. Mongooses can be killed by the venom of the cobras they prey upon. It is speed and agility that make the

In combat with a cobra, a mongoose will raise its stiff hair and rely on dodging tactics.

mongoose (as well as other predators) successful. The snake lacks the reserve of energy found in mammals and is quickly exhausted in a struggle. There are also skunks and opossums with antibodies in their blood that neutralize snake venom. Many other mammals devour nonpoisonous snakes: pigs, dogs, foxes, badgers and coyotes are some that regularly include snake meat in their diet. Predatory birds include eagles, owls, buzzards, road runners, hornbills and secretary birds. Snakes are not even safe from other snakes. King snakes, for instance, live almost exclusively on such dangerous fare as rattlesnakes and copperheads. Young snakes may at times even be swallowed whole by frogs.

But the greatest enemy of all is one who does not generally eat snakes — man. Fear and prejudice accounts for most snake killing by humans. Some people engage in this slaughter in an endeavor to protect domestic animals. Thus, an unremitting war on snakes has been pursued by man. Even more damaging, however, than the active attacks are the factories and large farms of man. The balanced ecological conditions necessary for a snake's well-being are invariably destroyed by man's ambitious works.

Snakes have no defense against the destruction of their environment. Those that cannot adapt, die. Against predators, they do have well-established defensive techniques. Usually, the first reaction to danger is to try to escape notice. A snake may lie perfectly still or withdraw to some suitable cover. If this maneuver should fail, snakes may display warnings — visual, auditory, or both. A chemical deterrent may be called into use. Only as a last resort will an attack be launched. Snakes that are startled, however, may be more immediately aggressive, as may those that are hungry or preoccupied with mating.

What defense does a snake have?

In hiding, snakes rely greatly on camouflage. Its color and pattern may blend with the background or else the arrangement of color may be so distracting that the snake's actual shape is lost to view. Desert species, therefore,

17

Secretary birds prey on snakes regularly.

are usually pale in color with light spots like sand grains. They may also have thornlike spikes above the eyes or on the end of the snout to disguise the outline of the head. Arboreal snakes are likely to be dappled, to harmonize with light and shadow, and to rest with the forepart of the body raised and bent so that they resemble twigs.

Visual warnings may consist of a sudden display of previously concealed colors and markings or an equally sudden change of shape and posture. Thus, snakes will raise themselves off the ground and inflate themselves. Some snakes have rounded tails that resemble their heads. These are waved to confuse a predator, so that the attack is made at the wrong end.

Although snakes have no voice, they are able to produce a sound by violently expelling air from the lung. Thus, we may hear a loud, startling hiss as a warning from an endangered snake. Many snakes, in addition to the rattlers, vibrate their tails to attract attention. Although they have no rattle, these snakes are able to beat a tattoo on the ground or rustle the vegetation beneath them.

Most snakes have a pair of sac-like glands inside the cloaca that produce scent. This is secreted through the vent when the snake feels molested. It can be extremely foul-smelling and certainly acts as a deterrent to predators.

Even when the last resort has been reached, the snake will hold back. The first lunges usually fall short of their object. After this display, a snake will frequently uncoil in preparation for a speedy withdrawal if the offender is rebuffed. But when all-out attack finally develops, it is fierce. Snakes that would ordinarily only bite and then release a hunting victim will bite repeatedly and with great force when defending themselves. Venomous snakes, of course, have the most formidable weapons. Some are even able to spit venom from a distance. The venom of snakes is the product of paired glands in the mouth. Grooves run from each gland to the fangs which are perforated. Several sorts of venom are produced by various species: some may cause disintegration of the body tissues, some prevent the blood from clotting, and some act on the nerves of the respiratory system and the heart. Large, constricting snakes, in their final defense, coil themselves around their adversary, suffocating it.

Kinds of Snakes

There is such an enormous variety of life that scientists

How do we count the kinds? have found it necessary to devise a sort of filing system to determine the relationships among forms. This is a convenient help to all of us who would like to know about animals. For instance, if we want to know the position in nature of a pet hognose snake, we could go about it as follows:

We have already established that snakes are reptiles closely related to lizards. This places our hognose in the order *Squamata,* which includes all snakes and lizards. Narrowing it down a bit, we find that snakes have a suborder all their own: *Serpentes* (formerly *Ophidia*). But there still remains an almost infinite variety: tree snakes, water snakes, burrowing snakes and terrestrial snakes; big snakes, small snakes, tropical snakes and snakes that live in temperate regions; snakes that lay eggs and snakes that bear live young. Where do we start? Well, we find that the next grouping has to do with families, animals that are much more closely related. In our pet's family, for instance, the *Colubridae,* we find many kinds of common snakes sharing certain characteristics special to them. Now we break it down into subfamilies, of which there are six. Our hognose belongs to the largest, the Colubrinae, which also includes such attractive members as garter snakes, corn snakes, and green snakes. We see that even within subfamilies, the differences are many, so we move further into genera. Here we find just one, *Heterodon,* which is the hognose. Checking up, however, we see that there are three species within the genus. They all look somewhat similar, being quite stocky (for a snake) and bearing the typical upturned nose. We must look closely to spot the differences. We find these mostly in the nose. Our snake's nose is less turned up than either of the others'. Thus, we know our pet to be the eastern hognose, *Heterodon platyrhinos.*

If we were to single out all the snakes in a like manner, we would come up with ten families, over 385 genera, and about 3,000 species. In many instances, scientists are not in complete agreement as to what constitutes a species of snake. It is sometimes difficult to fit each snake neatly into a man-made category. It may be that as the snakes are studied more fully, fewer species will be named.

Even in the larger grouping — families — all are not in agreement. Some zoologists think that seasnakes and cobras belong to a single family. There are those that believe that the vipers and pit vipers should be split into two distinct families and that the boas and pythons should have their separate families. More information on the evolution of snakes will ease the conflicts about family groupings. Until such information is complete, however, ten families in all represent the thinking of a majority of zoologists.

The Smaller Families

What are blind snakes?

Blind snakes are primitive burrowing snakes, strange in appearance, until one considers their underground habits. These reptiles, looking much like worms, are completely cylindrical, with small heads and short, rounded tails that resemble the heads. The eyes are tiny, with no spectacle, and are concealed by large overlapping scales of the same type that form the covering of the rest of the body. These are uniform in shape and size, with those of the belly exactly like those on the sides and back. The front of the head has a single plate forming a shield for pushing through the earth.

Within the body, these snakes show equally odd features. There are remnants of hind legs and a rigid skull that is shortened and consolidated.

These blind burrowers belong to the family Typhlopidae, which includes almost 200 species found in most warm parts of the earth, where they live quietly below ground, eating insects.

How does the thread snake differ from the blind snake?

Thread snakes (sometimes called slender blind snakes) form a small family of about 40 species known as the *Leptotyphlopidae*. They live mainly in semi-arid regions in Africa, Asia, North America and South America. Two species are found in the United States. They appear similar to blind snakes, but are smaller and thinner. They have all of their teeth in the lower jaw, however, while the blind snakes have theirs in the upper jaw. Thread snakes have a well-defined pelvis. A thigh bone may be seen as an external spur beside the vent.

Thread snakes thrive on termites and use termite nests as safe egg-laying places. They rarely emerge from below ground, except in the early evening when they may come to the surface for a brief period before dark.

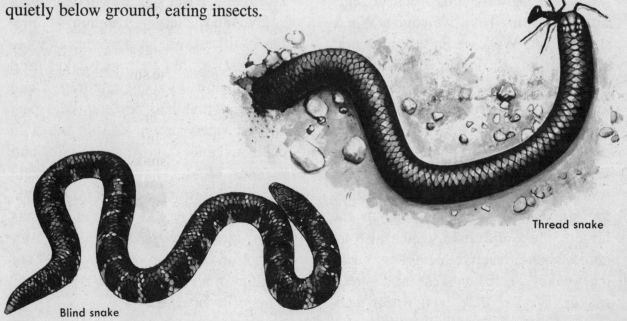

Thread snake

Blind snake

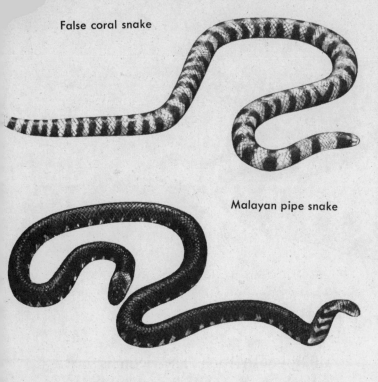

False coral snake

Malayan pipe snake

Shieldtails are burrowers, less than a foot in length, forming a family called Uropeltidae. Forty species living in India and Ceylon comprise the group. As their name implies, these snakes bear a large, shield-like scale at the back of the tail. No one knows exactly how this odd tail functions, but it is guessed that the coarse shield may plug up entrances to the snake's burrow. Perhaps, too, the tail is useful in locomotion, gripping the soil as the rest of the body straightens out.

What is a shieldtail?

Shieldtail snakes eat worms and other soft creatures. Many are brightly colored with red, orange, black or yellow in striking combinations. Unlike thread snakes and blind snakes, shieldtails do not lay eggs but give birth to live young.

Which snakes have claws on their bellies?

Three genera of snakes belonging to the family Anilidae bear tiny claws as vestiges of hind limbs. They are less primitive than the blind snakes, however, as they have small belly shields and spectacles covering the eyes.

One genus, *Anilius,* or the false coral snake, is found in South America. *Cylindrophis,* the pipe snake, lives in Ceylon; and *Anomochilus* is found only in Sumatra and Malaya. All are burrowers with cylindrical bodies, small heads and short tails. They eat eels and other snakes up to a foot long. All bear live young.

What is a sunbeam snake?

The family Xenopeltidae includes only one genus with a single species, *Xenopeltis unicolor,* living in southeast Asia. Although a dull brown in color, this snake has highly iridescent scales that shimmer brilliantly in certain lights.

The sunbeam snake has no trace of limbs or pelvis. The small head has typical snake shields covering it, but the jaws are immobile and the skull is compact for pushing into the earth. Sunbeams eat frogs, snakes and lizards.

Shieldtail

Sunbeam snake

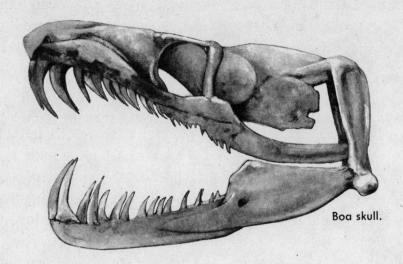

Boa skull.

Boas and Pythons

Boas and pythons, forming the family Boidae, are more primitive than the majority of living snakes. Their bodies have changed less from the old lizard pattern of their forebears. Thus, they have a pelvic girdle and hind limbs. (These, however, are very tiny and take no part in locomotion.) The pelvic girdle is not attached to the backbone and the legs (found only in males) are only single bones, covered by a horny claw that projects in front of the cloaca. There are two well-developed lungs, with the right one larger. The jaw retains a remnant of a bone found in lizards and not in other snakes.

How do boas and pythons differ from other snakes?

This family includes the real giants among snakes. Thus, it is easier for them to move by rectilinear creeping. Those species that climb have a prehensile tail for hanging onto branches, a useful appendage in a heavy snake. None of this group is poisonous — all kill by constriction. The victim is seized with the teeth, while the snake coils its body around that of the prey. Then it hangs on and squeezes. Death comes to the victim by suffocation, not crushing. The snake then swallows it whole.

Pythons have a bone in the roof of the skull that is absent in the boas. Boas bear live young and pythons lay eggs. The geographic ranges of the two groups are also distinct. Consequently, these snakes are divided into subfamilies.

How do the boas differ from the pythons?

Snakes belonging to the subfamily Boidae are found mostly in Central and South America, where there are over thirty species. There are also ten burrowing species in western Asia and North Africa. Three species of boa live on Madagascar and five inhabit Pacific islands.

Where do the boas live?

The most familiar of all the boas is the boa constrictor (*Constrictor constrictor*) of the American tropics.

What are some of the best-known boas?

It reaches fourteen feet in length and is extremely adaptable, being found in tropical rain forests as well as arid lands. Some have even made their way into the United States, hiding between bunches of bananas shipped in by boat.

The range of boa constrictors is very large, including the area from Mexico clear down to northern Argentina. The largest specimens come from Central America, but these are less visually attractive than smaller, more southerly types, as they are dark with markings less defined.

Central American boa constrictors are less even-tempered than those in South America, so make poorer pets. The main food is rodents, but ocelots, birds, and lizards are also consumed.

The rainbow boa (*Epicrates cenchris*) is almost as popular as the boa constrictor. Although many boas and pythons have iridescent skin patterns, none is more striking than that of the rainbow boa. This lovely reptile lives in areas from Costa Rica to Argentina. It is a small boa, reaching a length of about four feet. Although rather slow-moving, it can climb well, and after scouring the ground in search of its usual meal of rodents may take to the trees to catch a sleeping bat. A strong prehensile tail helps in the climb.

Boa constrictor

Rainbow boa

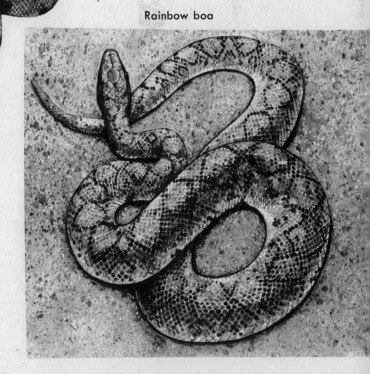

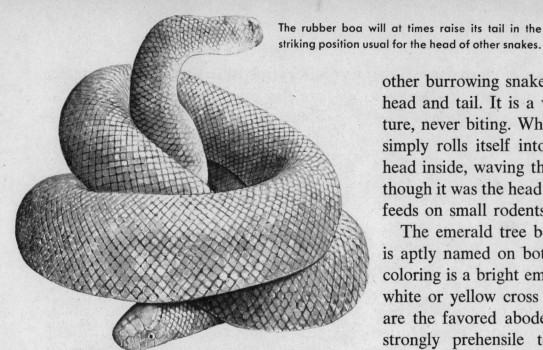

The rubber boa will at times raise its tail in the striking position usual for the head of other snakes.

A native of North America, the rubber boa *(Charina bottae)* can be found in humid areas from central California through the Rocky Mountains and into Montana and southwestern Canada. It inhabits evergreen forests. It owes its name to its rather rubbery appearance, but some admirers call it the silver boa, because of its rich color. Never exceeding eighteen inches in length, it spends most of its time underground. Like other burrowing snakes, it has a blunt head and tail. It is a very gentle creature, never biting. When threatened, it simply rolls itself into a ball with its head inside, waving the stumpy tail as though it was the head. The rubber boa feeds on small rodents and lizards.

The emerald tree boa *(Boa canina)* is aptly named on both counts. Adult coloring is a bright emerald green with white or yellow cross bands. Treetops are the favored abode and the tail is strongly prehensile to accommodate this habitat. Tree boas are about six feet long and fill their bulk with birds, squirrels and iguana lizards. When emerald boas coil themselves in the branches, they are effectively camouflaged. They bear long, strong front teeth that guarantee capture on the first strike.

Young emerald tree boas are not emerald at all. They are yellow or pink with white markings.

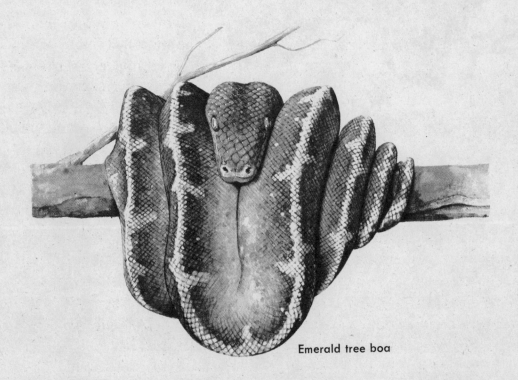

Emerald tree boa

The anaconda may grow to as long as 29 feet. It is the largest snake in the New World.

Cuban boa

Largest of all the snakes in Cuba is the Cuban boa *(Epicrates angulifer)*, which grows to about ten feet in length. At one time, it grew to be larger — almost fourteen feet — but these big specimens are now rare. The main food of this big boa is bats. Like its prey,

the Cuban boa is nocturnal. There are sensory pits in its lips which function as heat detectors — useful devices for a creature hunting warm-blooded prey after dark.

The real giant of the Boidae is the anaconda *(Eunectes murinus)*, reaching a length of 29 feet with a bulky body that may be three feet in girth. The anaconda ranges from the Orinoco Basin through the Amazon and the Guianas. It is a creature of the rivers, though not an especially good swimmer. Thus, it feeds less on fish than on the animals of the river banks. It lurks near water's edge with just eyes and nostrils above water, ready to capture mammals and birds walking down for a drink. It may dine on capybara, peccary, tapir, dog, sheep or pig. In some parts of its range, it overpowers the caiman (a kind of South American alligator). If disturbed by a human, an anaconda will submerge.

25

While some boas live in the water and some hang from trees, others lead a subterranean existence. There are the sand boas of the genus *Eryx*. There are seven species of sand boas living in arid parts of the Middle East and North Africa, and two others in the sandy soil of Asia, all small snakes, none exceeding three feet in length. The body is as well suited to burrowing as the tree boa's is to climbing. The head is short and strong with narrow nostrils that close to keep out the sand. An enlarged scale on the snout aids digging operations. Thus equipped, the sand boas fairly swim through the sand in search of subterranean lizards that are their prey.

The family Pythoninae is widely distributed over the globe with the exception of the New World.

Where do the pythons live?

Members can be found in Africa, southeast Asia, Malaysia and the Philippines. There are even a few scattered species on some Pacific islands and in Australia.

Brown sand boa

The reticulated python has the greatest length of all snakes.

The reticulated python *(Python reticulatus)* is world-famous as the longest of all snakes. It has been known to reach a length of 32 feet, and legends reporting much greater footage are still current. Unlike most snakes, reticulated pythons show no particular love of privacy and are happy to inhabit heavily populated cities in Asia, where they feast upon domestic livestock, as well as the rats that accompany mankind.

Which are the most familiar pythons?

Although the reticulated python is large enough to kill and eat a man, it rarely does so.

Like all pythons, the reticulated python mother lays eggs and incubates them. She will push them into a heap, then coil around them. She remains in this position with her eggs until they hatch about eighty days later, with only brief absences to obtain water.

The reticulated python lives near water and is an excellent swimmer, which accounts for its presence on many islands.

The Indian python *(Python molurus)* is the most common python of southern Asia. It frequents water habitats and can remain submerged for more than thirty minutes. It is also an excellent

A leopard falls victim to an Indian python.

The Indian python, like the reticulate, has a bold pattern of dark brown against light brown. Twenty feet is a maximum length.

The ball python *(Python regius)* of West Africa is a pet in a number of places, as it is small and gentle, and derives its name from its characteristically defensive reaction. It curls itself tightly, with head tucked inside. The ball formed is so uniformly round that it can be rolled along any flat surface.

The green tree python *(Chondropython viridis)* of New Guinea is similar in appearance to the emerald tree boa. The leaf-green color, prehensile tail and resting posture are almost identical in the two snakes. Young green tree pythons, like the American emerald tree boas, are not green. They are usually red at birth, changing later to yellow and finally to green. Green tree pythons reach an average length of seven feet.

The Australian python *(Morelia argus)* is sometimes called a carpet python. This is when it appears as a light brown snake with dark brown markings. When it is bluish black with large diamond-shaped markings, it is called the diamond python.

climber and is often found hanging by its prehensile tail from a convenient limb. From there it strikes at any warmblooded prey within range. The Indian python is afraid of few opponents and may even make a meal of a leopard. It rarely attacks a human, although people frequently eat this python, whose meat is reported to be delicious.

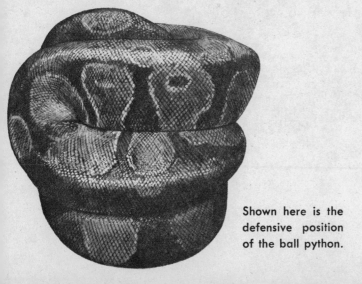

Shown here is the defensive position of the ball python.

Green tree python

Diamond python

This python is abundant in Australia and New Guinea. It can be found in trees, on the ground, and in the water. It is an especially valuable rodent-catcher and, as such, it is frequently kept in barns or granaries to control these pests.

The burrowing python or Calabar ground python *(Calabaria reinhardti)* is a subterranean snake living in the rain forest of west and central Africa from Liberia throughout the Congo. It grows only to three feet or so, and has the cylindrical body, smooth scales, blunt head, and short tail associated with burrowers. Under loose soil and leaf mold, this little python finds refuge. Above ground, it holds its head pointed down and keeps its tail up. From time to time, the tail sways, looking much like a normal snake head. Some people living in the area believe this to be a two-headed snake and give it a wide berth.

Calabar ground python

Typical Snakes

What is a colubrid?

The family Colubridae consists of three-quarters of all the genera of snakes in the world. All the typical, common snakes belong to this family — as well as several fascinating specialized species. Colubrids have adapted to many habitats. There are those that live on the ground, some under the ground, some above it in trees, and others that are aquatic. Most are harmless to man.

Colubrid snakes have only one lung and no trace of limbs or pelvis. Almost always a single row of scales covers the belly. There are usually nine enlarged scales shielding the upper part of the head. The lower jaw has only two bones on each side. Both jaws are very mobile.

Which are the most familiar colubrids?

The most well-known of all snakes belong to the subfamily Colubrinae. The northern water snake *(Natrix sipedon sipedon)* is one of eleven species found commonly in North America. It lives in fresh water where it feeds on fish, frogs, tadpoles, crayfish and salamanders. It is a highly patterned snake with black and brown markings against a lighter foreground with the colors standing out more clearly when the snake is submerged. Although not poisonous, the northern water snake is aggressive. Its bite is painful. This snake gives birth to live young, although its water snake cousins from the Old World lay eggs.

One of the Old World water snakes is the viperine *(Natrix maura)* living in France, Spain, Italy, northwest Africa, and several Mediterranean islands. If a viperine is disturbed on the ground, it will dash for the nearby water immediately. Occasionally, large numbers of viperines will congregate on river banks. Their food is much the same as that of American water snakes.

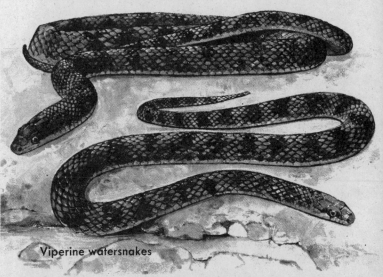

Viperine watersnakes

Eastern garter snake

San Francisco garter snake

Garter snakes are the most common of all North American snakes, indigenous to meadows, forests and swamps. In the suburbs, they are found in gardens; and in cities, in vacant lots. The eastern garter snake *(Thamnophis sirtalis)* has a ground color of black, brown or green, with stripes of yellow or green. The San Francisco garter snake *(Thamnophis sirtalis tetrataenia)* has showy red stripes.

Corn snake

The young are live-born in the summer, about six or seven inches long. At maturity, they reach two feet in length.

Garter snakes feed on earthworms, insects, toads, salamanders, small mammals, and birds. They also eat creatures of the water — fish, crayfish and frogs. Most species live near water.

The corn snake *(Elaphe guttata)* of the southeastern part of the United States is a truly beautiful reptile. Its warm brown, red, and yellow colors seem to vibrate in their patterns. Averaging three feet in length, it may on occasion reach six feet.

All snakes of the genus *Elaphe* are alternately referred to as "rat snakes" or "chicken snakes," in deference to their food preferences. While very important to us as rodent catchers, these snakes do also play havoc with our prize poultry. All kill by constriction.

The black rat snake *(Elaphe obsoleta)* is larger than the corn snake, reaching a maximum of eight feet. It lives in the northeast United States, usually in wooded areas. Its food may be birds, eggs, mice, rabbits, opossums, or lizards. It is partly arboreal, some specimens having been seen twenty feet up in trees. It wedges its body between the ridges of bark and hitches upward, aided by keeled scales along its belly.

The Aesculapian snake *(Elaphe longissima)* is a related snake, living in Europe and Asia Minor. This constrictor grows to about five feet in length and feeds on mice, rats and lizards. It is a good climber and frequents wooded areas, although it does sometimes invade farm buildings.

Black rat snake

This snake is the one used as the symbol of the Greek god of medicine, Aesculapius. It has been highly revered because of this association and transported to many parts of Europe as a token of health.

The northern black racer *(Coluber constrictor)* is one of several species of long, slender snakes reputed to be extremely swift. It is a dark blue-black with splashes of white on chin and throat. Its quick movements can be observed in tree branches as well as on the ground.

Racers feed on small mammals, birds, and frogs, lizards and other snakes. If threatened, a racer may vibrate the tip of its tail through dry vegetation, pretending to be a rattlesnake. If really provoked, it will bite vigorously.

Aesculapian snake

Northern black racer

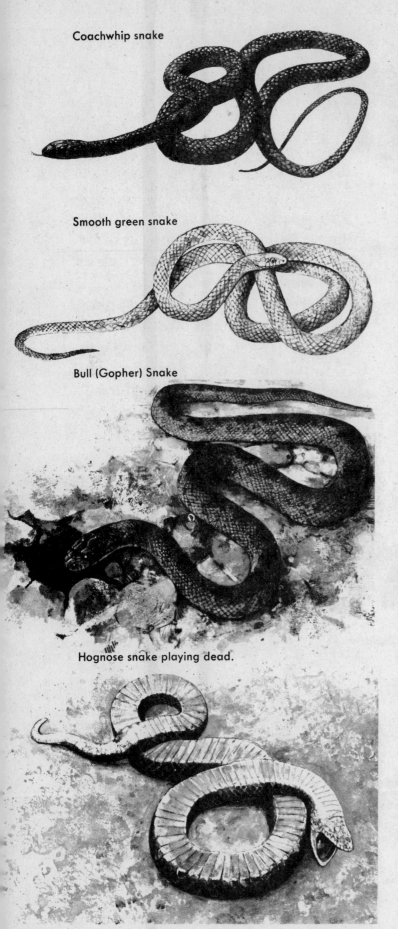

Coachwhip snake

Smooth green snake

Bull (Gopher) Snake

Hognose snake playing dead.

The coachwhip snake *(Masticophus flagellum)* inhabits the southern portion of the United States and Mexico in dry, open areas. There is a legend that the coachwhip ties men to trees with its coils, then whips them to death with its tail. As this is not a constricting snake and its average length is four feet, it is difficult to understand how the legend began. The coachwhip will bite repeatedly if disturbed. Food items include insects, small mammals, lizards, and even rattlesnakes.

The smooth green snake *(Opheodrys vernalis)* is very common in the United States and southern Canada, but because of its small size and excellent camouflage is rarely seen. It is only about fifteen inches long and quite slender. Smooth green snakes live in fields and marshes where they feed on spiders and insects. They are egg-layers.

Bull snakes of several species belong to the genus *Pituophis*. They all bear an enlarged scale on the snout for ease in burrowing. One species of the western United States is called a gopher snake, since it feeds on pocket gophers. In addition to gophers, bull snakes also eat mice, rabbits, and ground squirrels, making local farmers very happy, since this diet saves their produce. Bull snakes have a special membrane at the entrance to their windpipes. Thus, a bull snake's hiss is unusually loud.

The small eastern hognose snake *(Heterodon platyrhinos)* gets its name from its upturned snout, which assists in digging, as does its hard skull. Thus are toads removed from their burrows, as well as insects.

The hognose snake lives in the dry, eastern portions of the United States where it has achieved fame with its odd defensive habits. When bothered, this snake distends its head and neck to twice normal size, hisses loudly, and strikes (with closed mouth). If still molested, the hognose will suddenly pretend terrible agony and "die."

The king snake *(Lampropeltis getulus)* is a favorite with people in the United States, in spite of the fact that it is extremely shy, avoiding humans whenever possible, and apt to be aggressive if encountered. The reason for its popularity is the king snake's preference for other snakes, particularly poisonous ones, in its diet. In almost one motion, the king snake strikes its prey, twines itself around the other snake's body, and kills by suffocation. Rattlesnakes are so terrified of this opponent that they do not assume their customary defensive position (head and neck poised for the strike) in an encounter. Instead, they lower the head and neck to the ground and try to swat with a loop of the body. Almost any defense would be futile. Even if the rattler bit, the king snake, with its immunity to venom, would probably win.

A king snake winds itself around a copperhead.

Of the same genus, the milk snake *(Lampropeltis doliata)* is equally shy and retiring. Unlike the king snake, it is not a snake-eater, preferring small mammals. Although it was once believed that this snake drank milk from cows, there has been no evidence to substantiate this. It does, however, frequent barns in search of rodents.

The ring-necked snakes *(Diadophis)* of the United States and Mexico are easily recognized by their coloring. Slate-gray backs with yellow, red, or orange ring around the neck, and bright belly of yellow, orange or red make them stand out, although they are quite small. Living under stones or rotting logs in moist forests, the ring-necks spend most of their time hunting for insects and worms.

The vine snake *(Thelotornis kirtlandi)* of Africa is, as its name suggests, well adapted for life in trees. Its slender shape and camouflaging color allow it to resemble a vine. This snake can recognize stationary prey. A groove down the snout and a keyhole-shaped pupil that can extend along it allow it to see well in front when hunting or climbing.

Young milk snake

33

Vine snake

There is a subfamily of colubrids, quite different from the Colubrinae. These snakes, mostly of tropical regions, bear poison apparatus. They are the Boiginae. Enlarged teeth at the back of the upper jaw bear grooves through which poison produced in venom glands can trickle.

What are rear-fanged colubrids?

The venom gland of a rear-fanged snake is shown in this picture.

To use the fangs, these snakes must open their mouths very wide. None of the Boiginae are constrictors. The Montpellier snake, the black-and-yellow mongrove snake, the long-nosed tree snake, the boomslang, and the flying snake are all members of this group. The Montpellier snake is primarily terrestrial, preying on small mammals such as voles and rats. The others are arboreal, feeding on birds and lizards. Only the boomslang is dangerous to man, possessing a venom stronger than that of cobras and adders. It rarely strikes humans, however, preferring to save its

Chameleons and geckos are preferred prey. The vine snake has a colorful tongue (yellow, vermilion, or scarlet) with a black tip. This functions as a lure when it is flickered.

34

Flying snake

poison for prey. Most interesting of the group is the flying snake which glides from branch to branch. It jumps into space, spreading its ribs and flattening its body. This draws the undersurface in, making it concave. The snake actually forms a "parachute" of its body that slows its fall and allows it to glide a considerable distance.

Snail-eating snake

One subfamily of colubrids, the Dipsadinae, consisting of seventy species, make their living by eating snails. To accomplish the feat of pulling the animal from the shell, certain anatomical adaptations have taken place. The lower jaw is much longer than the upper, in some instances as much as three times as long. Only four or five small teeth are in the upper jaw. The snake bites the snail at the head, leaving the upper teeth holding on firmly, then works the long lower jaw into the shell. The lower teeth then sink into the prey, which is then pried out with a twisting motion. In addition to the odd jaw arrangement, snail-eaters are also different in that there is no fold of skin in the lower jaw, since there is no need for expansion when the prey is so small.

How do snail-eating snakes differ from other colubrids?

All snail-eaters are small, rarely reaching three feet in length. They are nocturnal and have very large eyes for seeing in the dark. They live in tropical America, southeastern Asia, and the East Indies.

The snail-eaters found one way to reject unwanted food containers. Egg-eaters have an entirely different means of accomplishing the same task. The mouth and neck are almost unbelievably stretchable, so the egg may be swallowed whole as far as the neck, where sharp projections on the vertebrae form a "saw." With swallow-

How does an egg-eating snake deal with its food?

ing motions, this saw cuts into the shell. The contents of the egg then spill into the stomach, while the shell is spit out through the mouth.

Egg-eating snakes which form this subfamily (Dasypeltinae) live mainly in Africa, with one species in India. They are small, arboreal snakes, searching the branches for birds' eggs. Like the snail-eaters, they are egg-layers.

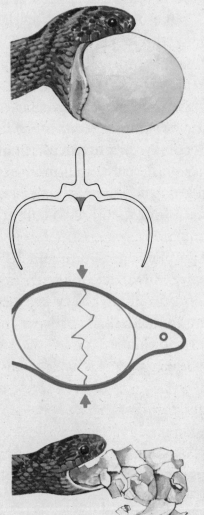

Egg-eating snakes use a sharp projection on the vertebrae to pierce the egg. The shell in then expelled in due time.

What are the specializations of some aquatic colubrids? Some aquatic snakes are so different from other snakes in their adaptation that scientists are in doubt as to their relationship. Although these are frequently placed in the subfamily Acrochordinae, some believe they deserve a family of their own.

The elephant trunk snake (*Acrochordus javanicus*) is one of this group. It lives in India, southeast Asia, and New Guinea and Australia. The name is derived from its very loose, wrinkled skin. There are closable nostrils located on the top of its head.

Another sort of aquatic colubrid is the fishing snake. *Herpeton tentaculatum,* from Indochina, spends its entire life in the water. *Herpeton* has two rear fangs with enough venom to kill fish and frogs, but has never bitten a human. This fisherman has two tentacles on its snout that are waved as lures to tempt fish.

Tentacles on this aquatic fishing snake lure fish.

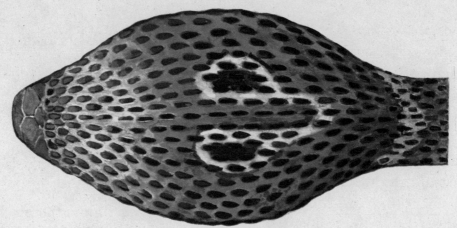

Eye markings are shown on this inflated cobra neck.

Cobras

What is a cobra? Cobras belong to the family Elapidae. They are poisonous snakes with fangs located at the front end of the upper jaw. These fangs are rigid and so they are always erect and ready for biting. The venom runs from the gland down through a tube in the tooth. Most cobras lay eggs and some species care for eggs and nest. With long, movable ribs in the neck region, some cobras are able to expand their necks into hoods, giving them a frightening appearance.

Where do elapids live? Members of this family can be found in all the warm regions of the world. In Australia, nine out of every ten species of snakes belong to the cobra family.

Which are the best-known cobras? The cobra with the best-developed hood is the Indian cobra (*Naja naja*). Although relatively small (four to five feet long), this cobra is particularly dangerous to man. This is because of its predilection for rats, which so frequently live in or near human houses. There is relative safety for people during the day, because Indian cobras see better at night and only then become far more aggressive. Cobra babies are even more belligerent than their parents and are able to rear, spread hoods, and strike even as they emerge from the egg. Indian cobras are devoted parents (for snakes), with male and female frequently remaining together to guard the nest until the young hatch.

The king cobra (*Ophiophagus hannah*) is the giant of the cobras, with the largest reaching 18 feet in length. Found over most of southeast Asia, it is, nevertheless, not common. This snake does its hunting by day and is as comfortable in the water or in trees as it is on the ground. Its game is other snakes — harmless or poisonous. It may even eat members of its own species.

The king cobra is one of the most aggressive of all snakes, attacking without provocation. It is also the only

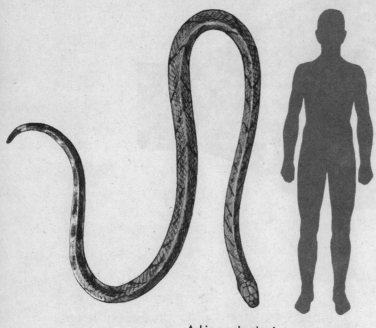

A king cobra's size, compared to that of the average man.

Egyptian cobra

Black-and-white cobra

Black-necked cobra

cobra to build its own nest for eggs. Parents remain together until the eggs are hatched.

The Egyptian cobra (*Naja haji*) of arid Africa feeds primarily on toads. It can grow to eight feet, but is not especially troublesome to people.

The black-and-white cobra (*Naja melanoleuca*) and the black-necked cobra (*Naja nigricollis*) share the same range in Africa, south of the Sahara Desert to Angola, but the black-and-white prefers forests, while the black-neck lives in the savanna. Neither is aggressive toward men. The black-and-white feeds on fish and frogs, and the black-neck on rodents and reptiles.

In the southern part of Africa lives the ringhals, a cobra that rarely finds it necessary to bite an enemy. The ringhals is able to exert muscular pressure against the poison glands so that a spray is ejected that may reach as far as eight feet. Since the ringhals aims for the eyes, fatality rarely follows, but acute pain and even blindness can result. Ringhals range from three to six feet and feed upon rodents, frogs, and birds' eggs.

The green mamba (*Dendroaspis angusticeps*) and the black mamba (*Dendroaspis polylepis*) can both be found south of the Sahara Desert in Africa. Black mambas are much larger, reaching a maximum of 14 feet, while the green rarely exceeds five. The black mamba is also more aggressive and, because it is very swift and has potent venom, deserves to be feared. Both species are good climbers; the green, with its camouflaging color, is particularly at home in trees. Black mambas feed on squirrels and birds, while the green mamba prefers lizards and birds.

Australia has a large and varied assortment of elapids. Many of them are extremely dangerous with very potent poison. Most of them bear live young. The Australian copperhead is one of the few snakes with a placenta.

The death adder is not an adder at all, but a cobra. It does resemble adders with its short, wide body, flattened head and spiked tail. Death adders come in a variety of colors — black, fawn, gray or red — to match the soil of their habitats. Well-camouflaged, death adders are more inclined to flatten themselves out and wait, rather than run from trouble. If stepped on, this three-foot cobra can inflict a serious bite. The spiked tip of the tail is frequently waved as a lure to lizards.

In southern Asia lives a small group of about one dozen species known as the kraits *(Bungarus)*. These are snake-eaters, feeding on venomous as well as harmless snakes. They are shy and un-aggressive toward man and will not bite unless severely provoked. Kraits are pretty, with scales so shiny they appear polished. Their eyes seem very large, because the iris is colorless.

Coral snakes are elapids found in North, Central, and South America. About 40 species exist. All have bodies with bands of contrasting color — red, black and yellow (or white). Some harmless snakes, such as the scarlet king snake, bear a similar color pattern and are difficult to distinguish. Although coral snakes are rarely aggressive toward humans, a bite could well be fatal.

Seasnakes

A small family of about 50 species, **What are seasnakes?** closely allied to cobras, are marine snakes. These reptiles (the Hydrophidae) have adapted well to the sea. Their bodies are flattened from side to side. Their tails, even more flattened, are used as oars. Nostrils close with a valve and turn upward. Most of them bear live young, so that they need not nest. Many have lost the large belly shields found in other snakes as a means of gripping the surface of the earth when moving.

Seasnakes are found in tropical seas. They are abundant along the coasts of Asia and Australia; but, oddly, are absent from the Atlantic Ocean. One species has made it as far as the west coast of the Americas and, in the other direction, all the way to Madagascar.

Although so well adapted to life in the ocean, seasnakes prefer shallow water and can sometimes be seen basking on the surface just off a coast.

The potency of the venom of seasnakes is unmatched by any other snake. Fortunately for us, seasnakes show no inclination to bite humans, reserving their poison for their prey, the fish of the seas.

Seasnakes are not very large — most are four or five feet long. They appear to be active both night and day.

Common European viper

The Vipers

What is a viper? A viper is the snake with the most highly evolved of all poison apparatus. Large poison glands add width to the head. Fangs are so long that they must be folded away when not in use. Vipers are so confident of their ability to hunt and defend themselves that they do not run from trouble or move quickly after prey. They simply lie in wait, strike their prey, and wait quietly for it to die. Because of this lazy way of life, vipers are somewhat stout. Most are terrestrial, inhabiting dry regions. No viper is aquatic.

There are two divisions in the viper family: the true vipers, or Viperinae, and the pit vipers, or Crotalinae. They differ in that pit vipers have a facial pit for sensing warm-blooded prey, while the true vipers do not. The highly poisonous true vipers inhabit most of Europe, Asia and Africa.

Which are the most common vipers? Ranging much farther north than any other snake is the common European viper (*Vipera berus*). It makes its home in such cold places as Scotland and Scandinavia and can even be seen within the Arctic Circle. There is notable variability in color and markings, but most of them have a dark V- or X-shaped mark behind the head. The common European viper is very hardy and emerges from hibernation as early as February. It feeds on lizards and voles. Normally, this snake is not dangerous to man, as it tries to avoid trouble.

Asp viper

Sand viper

Saw-scaled viper

Horned asp

Russell's viper

In some parts of its range, the European viper encounters the asp viper *(Vipera aspis),* and when this happens, the two may mate. (Hybrids have been seen.) The asp viper likes to lie buried in soft ground or sand with only its eyes and nostrils showing. It is active day and night, feeding on lizards, birds, and small mammals.

The sand viper *(Vipera ammodytes)* is identifiable by the small horn on its snout. It lives in the Balkan peninsula, northern Italy and southern Austria, in dry sandy areas where it spends much time lazing in the sun. This slow-moving snake possesses the most potent venom of any European viper and the most efficient poison apparatus. The fangs may be a half-inch long. The sand viper lives mostly on mice and voles.

One of the most dangerous of the vipers lives in southern Asia. This is Russell's viper *(Vipera russelli)* which, because of its large size (about 5½ feet) and strong poison, is one of the most feared of all snakes. It feeds mainly on rodents, but does not disdain frogs and lizards.

Close by, in Ceylon, then westward into Africa, lives the saw-scaled viper *(Echis carinatus)* with its bad temper. When bothered, this snake inflates its body, causing the saw-toothed scales to protrude. These it scrapes one against another to produce a wild, bubbling sound.

The horned asp *(Cerastes cerastes)* is a small snake commonly found in North Africa and Arabia. In this desert region the asp moves through the sand in a sidewinding manner. The keeled scales

42

are arranged so that, as the snake wriggles, the sand is thrown upward, quickly covering the animal. The asp can see when almost completely covered, as its eyes are directed upward. Over each eye is a sharp, pointed scale that protects the eyes from the strong sun and the shifting sands.

The puff adder *(Bitis arietans)* gets its name from its habit of inflating itself and hissing violently when annoyed. It is a large, thick-bodied snake, living on rodents. The fangs are extremely long and can be used as hooks for transport-

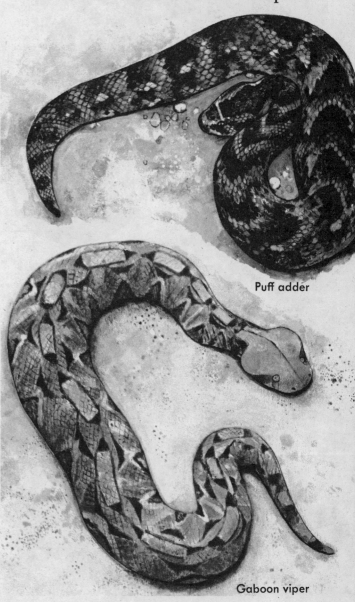

Puff adder

Gaboon viper

ing food to the mouth. It is a most dangerous snake.

The night adder *(Causus rhombeatus)*, on the other hand, is small and slim. It rarely uses its venom, even in catching prey. The frogs and toads it commonly feeds upon are simply seized and swallowed. Unlike most vipers, night adders have large shields (rather than tiny scales) covering the surface of the head.

Night adders are found in Africa south of the Sahara Desert, as are the Gaboon vipers *(Bitis gabonica)*. Although the Gaboon vipers have their eyes directed upward, like the puff adders, they are not desert snakes, but creatures of the tropical rain forest.

Gaboon vipers live on birds and mammals which they kill most efficiently with two-inch-long fangs and the most powerful of all viper poison.

The subfamily Crotalinae includes such

What is a pit viper? well-known vipers as rattlesnakes, copperheads and cottonmouths. These reptiles all possess special devices for sensing warm-blooded prey. There are small pits on the snout between the eyes and the nostrils. Actually, there is a large cavity at the front with a smaller one just barely visible above it. Between the two is a thin membrane supplied with heat-sensitive nerves. The stereoscopic effect resulting from the bilateral arrangement of the pits allows the snake to detect prey in the dark night with remarkable accuracy. Most pit vipers live in the New World, but there are also some in eastern Asia.

Views of the heat-sensitive facial pit: (top) side view—between eye and nostril; (bottom) head-on view.

American copperhead

Cottonmouth (water moccasin)

American copperheads *(Agkistrodon contortrix)* are

Which are the best-known pit vipers?

found in the eastern United States. They are relatively common in areas with plenty of cover.

Modest in its choice of food, the copperhead may content itself with caterpillars and cicadas, if mice and shrews are unavailable. The copperhead is somewhat retiring, but will bite if provoked. Many may retreat together to hibernate and may also accompany timber rattlesnakes in a den.

The cottonmouth *(Agkistrodon piscivorus)* of the southeastern United States is found in the vicinity of water, where it feeds on frogs, fish, and turtles. Cottonmouths demonstrate their annoyance by yawning. The white inside of their mouths names them.

The deadly fer-de-lance *(Bothrops atrox)* ranges from Mexico to Peru, wherever there are rats. Fer-de-lance venom is powerful and fast-acting.

Larger than the fer-de-lance is its neighbor, the bushmaster *(Lachesis muta)*. It can reach 12 feet in length. The bite is dangerous, but this is not a common snake and is unlikely to be encountered. Unlike other New World vipers, the bushmaster lays eggs rather than giving birth to live young.

As one might guess from its name, the jumping viper *(Bothrops mummifer)* hurls itself against its enemies. After coiling, this viper suddenly straightens up to deliver its bite, which, fortunately, is not too dangerous, as the poison is weak. The jumping viper lives in Central America and Mexico.

Fer-de-lance

Bushmaster

Jumping viper

Temple vipers in a Malayan temple.

Western diamondback rattlesnake

Pygmy rattlesnake

Although the temple vipers *(Trimeresurus wagleri)* of Asia are poisonous snakes, they are held in high regard by many people. On the island of Penang they are allowed the freedom of the temple. In parts of Borneo and Sumatra they are believed by many to bring good luck. These are climbing snakes with prehensile tails, living on birds and arboreal lizards.

There are about twenty species of rattlesnakes *(Crotalus),* most of which live in the United States. Like all other snakes, rattlers are deaf to airborne sounds, but nevertheless they have evolved a highly effective means of warning away enemies which do hear. The characteristic rattle is made by special scales at the end of the tail. These are hollow segments interlocking with each other. When the tail is moved, these hit against each other, providing a loud buzz. Rattlers may be found throughout the United States, as species are spread across the nation. The eastern diamondback is native to the southeast, the western diamondback lives in deserts and prairies from Mississippi to California. Timber rattlers are most common in the eastern states, while prairie rattlers live in western Canada as well as the United States.

The pygmy rattlesnake *(Sistrurus miliarius)* of the southeastern United States reaches only eighteen inches and has a less-developed rattle. It is, nevertheless, aggressive, while its relative, the massasauga rattler *(Sistrurus catenatus)* is gentler. The massasauga is found in the Midwest, from the Great Lakes to Texas.

Snakes and People

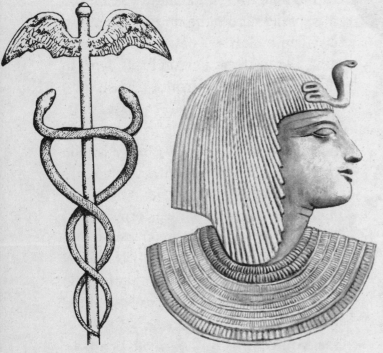

The sounds of the snake-charmer's flute aren't heard by the snake. The snake merely responds to the swaying movement.

The snake-entwined caduceus was the symbol of Mercury. Snakes were also featured on Egyptian headdresses.

Which people have made snakes godlike? Although people in modern times are frequently hostile toward snakes, many ancient people had great respect for them. The unusual qualities of snakes — the unblinking eyes, the legless movement, the ability to kill with a single bite — made some people regard snakes as gods. In Africa, Asia, North and South America, and Europe, snakes have been worshipped.

In Egypt, the goddess Buto was frequently represented as a cobra. This ruler of the rich delta was revered as a great protectress. India has many legends built around the Nagas, a magical race of snake gods. Some royal Indian families even claimed the Nagas as ancestors. Statues of these snakes are still worshipped in the south of India. In Mexico, Quetzalcoatl, a plumed serpent, was the god of wind, the creator of life, and the patron of the arts. The Hopi Indians of Arizona still do a snake dance to bring rain. Priests of the tribe hold snakes (even rattlers) in their mouths during this dance.

Snakes have also been the symbols of many peoples. The Aesculapian snake was used as the symbol of the Greek god Aesculapius, who was responsible for healing. This snake, twined around a staff, is used today as the emblem of the medical profession. In medieval times, organs of snakes were used to cure various diseases.

Whether hostile or worshipful, people remain fascinated by snakes. Their fear has prompted them to pay performers to demonstrate their mastery over poisonous species. Snake charmers have been popular entertainers for centuries.

How do snakes help us?

Snakebite now is not as disastrous as it used to be, because antidotes to most venom is now available. To secure the antidote, venom must be extracted from living snakes. These are kept on snake farms and used when needed. The venom of one viper has also been found to work as a coagulant to stop bleeding.

Many farmers know the value of snakes as rodent killers. In some places they are deliberately placed in grain storage bins to consume the rats drawn to this food.

Snakeskin has long been used as leather, since its texture and patterns are lovely. Snake meat is eaten by many people who consider it delicious.

One of the best ways to satisfy our curiosity about snakes is to keep one as a pet. Snake keepers become as attached to their charges as others to dogs, because snakes can be quite responsive to their handlers. It is not an easy job to keep a snake. It requires much time and patience.

How do we keep snakes as pets?

Setting up a home is the first major job. Before you bring your pet into the house, his home must be ready to receive him. The best enclosure is a glass terrarium, easily available through a pet shop. Be sure to obtain one large enough to house your snake in comfort. A ten-gallon tank is about right for an average-sized snake. You must also buy a heater or use a light bulb over the tank so that temperature can be controlled at the high level necessary to reptiles. A tight lid is an absolute necessity, for all snakes are outstanding escape artists. You may plant your terrarium, if you like, but this is a bit dangerous, since snakes must be kept dry, and the moisture from the floor of a woodland or bog-type terrarium could make your pet ill. Be sure to include branches for climbing so the snake can get up off the floor. If your choice is a small watersnake, a small pool should be constructed at one end of the tank. And there should be a private place so the snake can hide occasionally. Too much company or confusion makes a snake unhappy.

Once the home is ready, you may select your pet. Whether you are buying it in a pet shop or collecting from the wild, certain rules should be observed. The snake must be healthy when you get it. Look for one that is active. Sluggishness is frequently a sign of poor health. The snake's eyes should be bright and sparkling. No cysts, lumps, or blemishes should mar the beauty of the skin. These are all signs of illness. The snake should look fat. Tropical or exotic species are harder to keep. For a first pet, it is better to secure a common local species. Avoid venomous snakes. These are too dangerous to be satisfying pets and are, in any case, difficult to keep healthy.

"Milking" a snake for its venom.

Once your snake has adapted himself to his new home and is happily accepting food from your hand, you will be able to hold and fondle him. Place your hand on his neck just behind the head and lift gently, supporting the body with your other hand.

Feeding is the next hurdle. As snakes are carnivorous, you must furnish fresh meat of some kind. Live food is most satisfying to the snake. This may be anything from earthworms to guinea pigs, depending upon the size of your pet. If you object to seeing a live mouse swallowed, you can kill it before feeding. Most small snakes enjoy earthworms as food. Watersnakes can be given live goldfish in their pool and some also enjoy slugs. Hognose snakes eat toads, and frogs are a favored food of garter snakes. Green snakes are the easiest to feed, as they do well on crickets which may be caught in the summer and purchased during the winter. Most snakes can be trained, eventually, to feed on strips of fresh fish and beef.

Some snakes go on hunger strikes in captivity. If this happens, you have several alternatives. Native snakes can and should be released. Others may need more heat; try to adjust your heater appropriately. Perhaps feeding at another time of the day or night might promote more interest in the food. Different sorts of food can be tried. If all else fails, try force feeding.

Young children have little instinctive fear of snakes, but even a chimpanzee reared in a zoo will try to avoid a snake if confronted with it.